When I was a Boy... I Dreamed

Written by

Justin Matott

Illustrated by

Mark Ludy

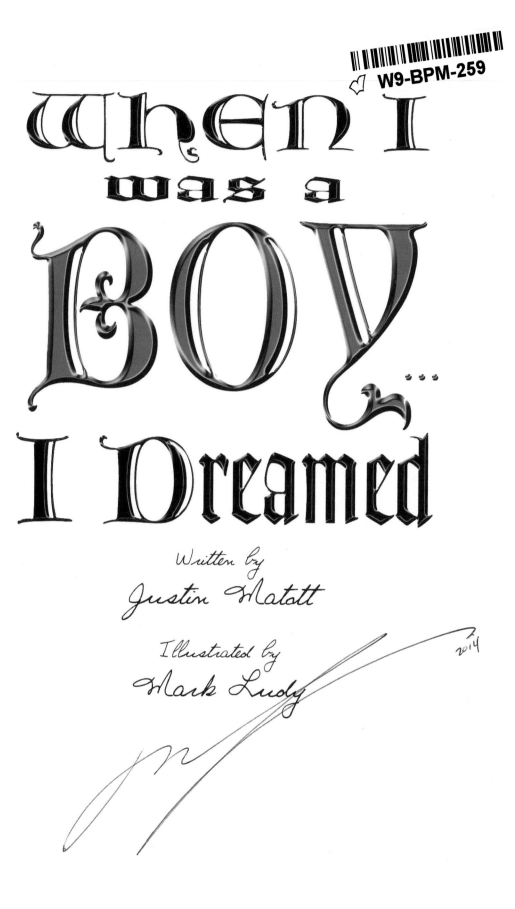

Scribble&Sons
GoodBookCo.com

When I was a boy...

I dreamed

Big Dreams!

I ventured far and near,

and dreamed of great exploring.

Of those dreams you will now hear...

I dreamed I lived up in a tree,

way above the earth below.

Not just in any sort of tree,

in a tree house you should know!

I dreamed I explored the jungles

for the rarest kind of beast,

fought off snakes and gorilla gangs

as I hunted for my feast.

I dreamed I dug to China,

burrowed 'till my back was sore.

And when I hit the other side,

met a Chinese man, then millions more...

I dreamed I built a rocket ship,

and made a spacey suit.

I blasted up... oh so high...

in my rocket I would shoot.

I banged and pieced together

all sorts of rocket parts.

I brought in steel and cushions;

I wheeled them in by carts.

I dreamed I found the treasure,

the end of the rainbow at last.

A Leprechaun guarded the pot of gold,

I had to think up something fast...

I dreamed I saved a maiden

captured by a dragon mean.

We fought and fought some more

as I battled for that future queen.

I dreamed of ocean battles,

on the high seas I was boss.

We'd hunt down evil pirates,

them off their bow I'd toss.

I chased off all those buccaneers,

the worst was Fearsome Frank.

In his stripey, little underwear,

I made him walk the plank!

I dreamed I ran an ice cream shop,

every flavor you could find.

And if it wasn't there, I'd create

whatever came into your mind!

I dreamed I was a hero,

a firefighter sure and brave!

I'd climb the highest ladder,

those in peril I would save!

I dreamed I built a submarine

to reach the deepest deep,

I'd explore the underwater world

for what may lurk and creep.

I brawled with an eight-legged beast

who fought with all his might.

We wrestled and we battled

for weeks, both day and night.

I dreamed I was a football star,

and touchdowns were my goal.

I played with all my heart and might!

The champion of the Superbowl.

I dreamed I was a one-man-band,

played each instrument you know...

Had crowds and fans at every stop

where I'd put on my show!

I dreamed I roamed the lonesome plains,

way out in the Old West.

In my cowboy jeans and fancy hat,

and my official sheriff vest.

I showed up there right at high noon

and stopped a robber cold.

He tried to hold up the bank,

but now he ain't so bold!

*W*ell, that's all the time we have for now.

I hope you enjoyed your stay.

Come on back sometime soon,

to hear of the whale I rode today.

*S*o many dreams and great adventures,

still for you to hear about!

But I will say, "So long, goodbye,"

yes, for now...

"over and out!"

For my sons., Dash & Canon
— Mark Ludy

For JJ & Ethan, my boys!
And to Alex, Eric, Kyle and Nick (my other boys)
— Justin Matott

Illustrator
MARK LUDY is the writer and illustrator of several books. With a style all his own he creatively reaches audiences everywhere, be it through his books, his art or his speaking. With a hilarious sense of humor he engages people of all ages. Mark is happily married with three children. Discover more about him and his new works at **MARKLUDY**.com

Author
JUSTIN MATOTT is the writer of many books including "When I Was A Girl... I Dreamed." He is a passionate soul who loves what he does and it shows. He is a regular speaker in schools and has the ability to communicate with kids in such a way that they "get it." Justin lives in Highlands Ranch, Colorado. Be sure to discover all Justin's book at **JUSTINMATOTT**.com

For information regarding permissions, write to SCRIBBLE & SONS @ INFO@GOODBOOKCO.com

2013 Paperback Edition

Scribble & Sons
www.GoodBookCo.com

Scribble & Sons is an imprint of Green Pastures Publishing , Inc.

Matott, Justin.
Ludy, Mark.
When I Was A Boy... I Dreamed/Justin Matott; illustrations by Mark Ludy
Summary: An old man tells of the extraordinary dreams he had as a young boy.
But were they dreams at all, or perchance tales from an amazing life still being lived
by an unassuming, little man with a cane...

ISBN-13: 978-0615932798
ISBN-10: 0615932797

Printed in USA
By CreateSpace

Other wonderful books by author/illustrator Mark Ludy

Scribble & Sons
GoodBookCo.com